SHARAF RASHIDOV

Kashmir Song

RASHIDOV ★ 100
CENTENNIAL CELEBRATION

To my Mother Maria Akhmedjanova who spent many years working with Sharaf Rashidov on developing his hometown Jizzakh in Uzbekistan

— Marat Akhmedjanov

HERTFORDSHIRE PRESS

Published in United Kindom
Hertforfshire Press Ltd © 2017

9 Cherry Bank, Chapel Street
Hemel Hempstead, Herts.
HP2 5DE, UK
e-mail: publisher@hertfordshirepress.com
www.hertfordshirepress.com

THE KASHMIR SONG by Sharaf Rashidov

Translation: Alexey Ulko
Editor: Robin Thomson
Illustrations: Aigul Khakimzhanova, Lesya Kara-Kotsya
Design: Aleksandra Vlasova

*British Library Catalogue in Publication Data
A catalogue record for this book is available from the British Library
Library of Congress in Publication Data
A catalogue record for this book has been requested*

ISBN: 978-0-9930444-2-7

CONTENTS

Post-Colonial Struggle and *The Song of Kashmir*
by Sharaf Rashidov

The proposal to translate Sharaf Rashidov's *Song of Kashmir* triggered in me a mixed response because of the ambiguity and complexity associated with this author. Rashidov, later to become First Secretary of the Communist Party of Uzbekistan and a member of the Central Committee of the Soviet Communist Party, and who was already the Chairman of the Presidium of the Supreme Council of the Uzbek SSR when he wrote *The Song of Kashmir* in 1956, had begun his career as a journalist, poet and writer. By the end of that career, however – having remained leader of Uzbekistan continuously from 1959 to 1983 – Rashidov had become a controversial figure. His name was linked to the so-called 'Uzbek case', a corruption scandal rooted in the fundamental flaws of the Soviet system in which the Kremlin singled Rashidov out as the ringleader and almost the sole suspect in the country while ensuring that the activities of the top authorities remained obscure. On the other hand, however, among the Uzbek people Rashidov was remembered as a folk hero who used his skill as a leader to 'beat the system' and brought many benefits to Soviet Uzbekistan.

A summary in Russian of some of Rashidov's major creative achievements goes as follows:

Rashidov's first collection of poems, called *My Anger*, was published in 1945. His novella *The Victors* (1951) depicts the people's labours to cultivate new arable lands. ... The heroes are found in the novel *Stronger than the Tempest* (1958) ... the novel *Mighty Wave* (1964) was devoted to the heroism of the Soviet people on the home front during the Second World War. The romantic novella *The Song of Kashmir* (1956) reflects the Indian people's struggle for liberation. In 1950 Rashidov published a collection of political articles, *The Verdict of History*, and in 1967 a book, *The Flag of Friendship*. Rashidov's critical articles focus on the topical issues in Soviet literature.

(*cited in Wikipedia article on Sharaf Rashidov, Russian version, as at 2014. My underlining*)

Judging by its tone, this summary of Rashidov's works and the reference in it to *The Song of Kashmir* date from Soviet times, and at first glance seem far removed from the genre or the content of the piece. The novella itself takes the form of a dramatic and florid retelling of a traditional Kashmiri legend about the cyclical change of seasons and the yearly triumph of the forces of life over the forces of death and decay. This narrative of natural wisdom is developed by the story of the all-conquering love between Bambur, the King of the Bees, and the spring narcissus, personified by Nargis and surrounded by other equally beautiful and life-loving flowers.

Their antagonists, the cruel Blizzard and the enigmatic bringer of death Harud, overwhelm the blossoming valley with their vile power but in the end are defeated, powerless against the love and the force of life embodied by the flowers, the bees, the trees and the sun shining down on the valley.

Although the metaphors of the ancient legend are clear and straightforward, there are two indications in the text that it may contain hidden meanings. The book opens with a cryptic dialogue between a master and his disciples about collective memory as the source of wisdom and ends with the author stating several possible interpretations of the *Song*. The distinction made by the master between 'watching' and 'seeking at length' is an allusion to Sufi teachings. The interpretations offered at the end, meanwhile, in addition to literal readings of the plot as a story of invincible love or as a profound metaphor of the natural cycles of death and resurrection, include the bold statement, yet scarcely substantiated, that the legend retold by Rashidov represents 'the struggle of the Indian people against the colonial yoke', the latter embodied in the text by the Blizzard and the life-sapping Harud. Since this interpretation indeed appeared in the literary encyclopaedias of the time, it evidently was part or all of the hidden meaning hinted at by Rashidov. So what were his motives for making such a point? It would take some research into the history of Indian postcolonial politics and the Cold War to find out. And as I embarked on this, a remarkable series of reminiscences and transformations, both political and literary, opened up.

When India gained independence of British colonial rule in 1947, Kashmir was still formally an independent state inhabited by Muslims, Hindu and Sikhs with the progressive Sheikh Muhammad Abdullah as one of its civil leaders. Lord Mountbatten of Burma, the last Viceroy of India, believed that Kashmir should be a part of India and not of Muslim Pakistan. In this he enjoyed the support of the Indian leaders Jawaharlal Nehru and Mahatma Gandhi, who sought to influence Sheikh Abdullah, and in due course the Sheikh became the first Prime Minister of Kashmir within the Union of India. By 1953, however, the situation had changed as the initial hopes for a peaceful coexistence between the Muslim, Hindu and Sikh communities were replaced by a growing awareness of fundamental differences between the communities. This was the time of escalating tensions between the Communist-bloc countries led by the USSR and the capitalist democracies, above all the USA. The Soviet Union was trying to consolidate its position and was looking for new allies in the Third World, while the USA was fighting the Korean War and the Second Red Scare was at its peak.

In August 1953 Sheikh Abdullah and a number of his associates were arrested by the Indian authorities, accused of conspiring with Pakistan (and thus also with the USA) against the Indian state with the aim of seceding from India and joining Pakistan. Nehru was apparently shocked when he saw the evidence of his former friend's scheming against India. The infamous Kashmir Conspiracy Case began and there were demonstrations and civil disturbances all over the country. Nehru managed to unravel the 'imperialist plot', however, and in 1955 the Soviet leaders Nicolay Bulganin and Nikita Khrushchev paid a triumphal visit to India, where they finally cemented the victory of the left-wing forces over the capitalist reactionaries. But what does all this have to do with *The Song of Kashmir*?

Among that large Soviet delegation to India was Rashidov, who attended a performance of the first opera in the Kashmiri language written by the poet Dinanath Nadim (a major figure of the Cultural Conference, a progressive writers' movement in Kashmir). The opera, *Bombur taa Yamberzal* (The Bee King and the Narcissus) was based on a traditional Kashmiri legend, radically re-worked by Nadim. According to Moti Lal Kemmu, a prominent playwright and theatre critic, who also took part in the performance, 'in our discussions "the 1953 episode" [the alleged conspiracy with Pakistan – *AU*] was attributed to imperialistic intrigue. Since the Cultural Conference was an organisation of progressive writers, artists, theatre people and performing artists, it promoted cultural programmes reflecting the unity of all peace-loving Kashmiris and exposing imperialistic manoeuvring'. Nadim decided to reflect this political position in his opera, which he created after a visit to China where the opera *The White Haired Girl* had made a strong impression on him. This, one of the eight model operas of revolutionary China, told the story of a peasant couple who are separated by enemy figures, only to be reunited after the protagonist joins the Chinese revolutionary army fighting the Japanese invaders. The reunion is made possible by victory over the enemy and, simultaneously, the overthrow of an evil landowner who had held the girl in captivity. The plot, which parallels the liberation of the motherland and that of the fiancée in an act of courageous resistance at both romantic and political levels, was created within Socialist Realism and also became a template for several Asian writers.

Inspired by the Chinese opera, Nadim decided to write a similar piece in Kashmiri. He drew on a folk legend as the basis but changed its ending to suit his purposes. In the original legend the King of the Bees turns blind searching for his beloved narcissus while she is withering in the sun, but Nadim created a new, optimistic finale and imbued it with topical political references. Now the antagonists were more personified and recognisable, as in the example of Harud, the enemy of living things (*harud* is the Kashmiri for autumn, the time of decay). Moti Lal Kemmu maintains that '*Bombur taa Yamberzal* was a symbolic opera. The flowers all represented peace-loving Kashmiris. Wav and Harud (*wind* and *autumn*) represented the agents of imperialism that divided people'. Nadim's opera was therefore deliberately created as a politically charged piece of art related to a specific political context, and that was how it was perceived by the Soviet delegation that attended its second production in 1955. The new Soviet government considered establishing stronger ties with India a priority to counter the growing US influence in the capitalist world, particularly in Pakistan, and the Kashmir dispute had been of major strategic significance in the struggle for regional domination. It is difficult to say now how the decision to translate the new version of the legend into Uzbek and Russian was taken, but there can be no doubt that it was sanctioned at the highest level of the Soviet hierarchy.

I was unable to obtain the original libretto to *Bombur taa Yamberzal*, which may not have survived, so can rely only on circumstantial evidence for whatever changes Rashidov may have made to it in his novella. It appears that he further stressed the antagonism between the good and evil forces. The final victory of the former is linked moreover to the coming of spring, and this ties the narrative to the symbolism of the ancient Central Asian festival of Nowruz (the traditional new year, the first day of which occurs on the vernal equinox), a festival also celebrated in Kashmir. Rashidov also gave Uzbek names to the flowers of the valley (Nargis the narcissus, which is traditionally associated with Nowruz, Lola the tulip and Atyrgul the rose), while leaving the name Harud untranslated, making it a more abstracted manifestation of the force of evil, one that wreaked its destruction in various ways and at various times. Additionally Rashidov sprinkled the prose text of the legend with a number of songs and poems that make references both to the verse in Nadim's opera and to the culturally familiar imagery of Uzbek poetry. By making these alterations, Rashidov was continuing the trans-cultural adaptation of the narratives of fighting for freedom that the Kashmiri poet had initiated.

The Song of Kashmir was published in Uzbek (*Kashmir qyshigi*) in 1956, shortly after the Soviet delegation to India; in 1958 it was translated into Russian, and in 1961 the Uzbek composer Georgy Muschel wrote a ballet based on the novella. In an article about the composer's life, Lilia Nikolenko wrote: 'The ballet was created out of [Muschel's] direct impressions of Sharaf Rashidov's poem *The Song of Kashmir*, which reflected a poetic Indian legend. The composer also wrote the libretto to the ballet, in which the common striving of the people of the East for independence and the triumph of peace and goodwill are manifested with power and passion.' With this ballet the legend, having passed through several transformations, returned to the stage.

It is interesting to see how the public discourse surrounding *The Song of Kashmir* gradually changed over time. Eventually it lost all reference to the opera *Bombur taa Yamberzal* and its significance for politics and society in Kashmir in the mid-1950s. Dinanath Nadim is mentioned only as a reteller of 'an ancient Kashmiri legend'. The politically significant identification of the Kashmiri and Indian cultures is taken for granted and the plot as presented by Rashidov now symbolises 'the common effort of the peoples of the East in their struggle for independence'.

Political and literary references and remakes of *The Song of Kashmir* continued to proliferate, using a growing range of media. In 1965 a cartoon *Nargis* was made in the USSR based on *The Song of Kashmir*. This version featured a *doppelgänger* motif and the dramatic death and resurrection of the protagonist. In 1967, twelve years after the first performance of *Bombur taa Yamberzal*, Dinanath Nadim's opera received the Sahitya Academi Award for its contribution to the development of Kashmiri literature. According to the Kashmiri writer and blogger Vinayak Razdan, 'in 1971, the Soviet government conferred on Nadim the Soviet Land Nehru Award, a prize given by the Soviet Union to selected Indian artists in recognition of their outstanding work.' In the late 1970s, in the context of growing tension between India and Pakistan, Rashidov, who by now had retired from literary work, re-published *The Song of Kashmir* with the additional commentary about the various possible interpretations of its plot. According to the Indian journalist Alok Shekhar, in 1984 Rashidov's novella inspired and informed the famous Soviet-Indian film *The Legend of Love* which in fact has more in common with the novel of the same name written by another great friend of the Soviet Union, the Turkish author Nazim Hikmet. In another curious twist, another major Asian writer, Salman Rushdie, gave the name Bombur Yamberzal to one of his characters in *Shalimar The Clown*, a novel about Kashmir and 'the politics of the sub-continent that ripped apart the lives of those caught in the middle of the battleground'.

To underline the inherent contradiction within the plot, Rushdie named Bombur Yamberzal's wife Harud, a small but remarkable touch of his postmodernist irony. The resilience and flexibility of the legend is indeed amazing. Finally, there is also evidence of the alleged importance of *The Song of Kashmir*'s translation into Hindi for Indian culture and the relationships between India and the USSR. In 2003, twenty years after Rashidov's death, Alok Shekar wrote: 'The world still remembers the great Uzbek poet and writer Sharaf Rashidov, who was the republic's leader for many years. He is admired not only in the former Soviet states but also abroad because his contribution to the world's treasury of literature and culture was great and impressive'. The true artistic significance of Rashidov's writing for world literature, of course, remains a matter of opinion, but there can be no doubt about its great political and social importance in a broader context.

The disintegration of the Soviet Union and of international communism and the resultant shift of political balance in the world has clearly had radical implications for art created within the Socialist discourse. It makes little sense to try to guess the possible reactions of Nadim or Rashidov to these developments – whether they would have seen them as a triumph of capitalism or a victory for the anti-colonial struggle of oppressed peoples. Yet this ambiguity and uncertainty itself throws some light on the issue of topicality in contemporary art, which is all too often interpreted in a narrow sense, reducing a work of art to the level of superficial satire. Nadim's opera and Rashidov's novella provide good examples of the way in which meanings are lost or abruptly skewed when the political circumstances under which they were created are changed. These events clearly show how easily snappy political tags can be changed and reapplied while the key problems faced by humanity remain unresolved. The publication of *The Song of Kashmir* in English may thus be viewed as a call for a further stage in the historic re-evaluation of various parts of the Central Asian literary heritage. In a wider context, however, it aids contemplation of the real significance of contemporary art in today's controversial world.

Alexey Ulko
Samarkand-Tashkent 2014

SHARAF RASHIDOV

Kashmir Song

A Novella

Author's Note

This tale is based on an ancient Kashmiri legend. It is still performed – narrated and sung – in Kashmir today, with music written by the gifted composer and teacher Dina Nath Nadim.

Sharaf Rashidov

Prologue

A teacher who had lived much, seen much and tasted much of joy and sadness asked his pupils, whose young eyes were keen and whose minds were just spreading their wings in preparation for a long flight, the following question:

'Where do the rivers begin?'

'In the mountains,' answered one.

'They begin as springs in the depths of the earth,' said another.

'In the seas and oceans,' replied a third.

The teacher waited a while to see whether there would be other answers, but the pupils were silent, so he said to them:

'Each of you has spoken the truth of appearances, but not the truth of essence. The truth of appearances opens to one who watches, and the truth of essence opens up to one who thinks and seeks at length. If you say that rivers take their being from mountains or springs, you forget that the water first came there from the seas and oceans. But someone who says that rivers are born of the seas and oceans has forgotten that the water reached the seas from mountains and springs. The one who claims to have found the beginning and the end, having discovered only one link of a chain and unaware that its ends are joined, is either deluded, an ignoramus or a liar.'

After thinking for a while the teacher again asked:

'And where does human wisdom originate?'

'In experience,' answered one pupil.

'In thought,' said another.

'From the joining of thought and experience,' replied a third.

Thinking again for a moment, the teacher then said:

'A man's experience dies together with the man and a man's mind dies together with the man. Our lifetimes are short! But wisdom originates in the memory of the people. It is an ocean that gives birth to mountain streams and springs; it is the ocean into which the springs and mountain streams flow, having meanwhile become rivers. Memory is an effect of wisdom and is also its cause. But where does that memory reside and what gives it the power to move and grow richer through the ages, from the times of the past to the times of the future?

'It is in a drawing on a rock or a painting on a canvas.

'It is in a line engraved on stone or in books.

'It is in a fairy tale, a legend, a tradition.

'It is in music and song.

'These are where the collective memory resides as it runs on from generation to generation, and these are where the human wisdom is gathered, which is passed from generation to generation like a torch that burns ever brighter.

'These are for us to receive, to carry in ourselves and to pass on!

'For us to add to one seed another seed and to one line another line, to one fruit another fruit and to one music another, to one flower another flower and to one song another song!'

I

Spring came carefree and fleet of foot to the wide valley that stretched from horizon to horizon.

The streams seemed like silver as they ran down the mountains and framed the valley; moving in smooth arcs, the river glittered gold, and the earliest, bravest and most impatient of the shoots had raised themselves and burst into flower. Imbibing all the colours of the sunrise and the sunset, the dew and the rain, the water and the sky, they danced in blue and yellow, pink and violet, lily and orange, some brighter than others and some more handsome than others; they smiled at the sun and the sun smiled on them. But when they needed rest from the intense heat, snow-white clouds came and shaded them with their racing shadows.

Birds were flying about in great numbers, singing their songs in their countless modes. What were they singing of? Nobody could ever have expressed it in words, but everybody knew that it was the joy of living and the song of life, a language understood by all. And above the shimmering colours and the birdsong rose the silent high mountains of the valley sides, perpetual snows on their peaks.

First to bloom in the valley was Nargis.[1] Her beauty was

---

1 *Nargis - Narcissus*

incomparable with anything, and anybody who saw her even once would remember her for ever. Wearing a blue velvet jacket over a silk dress, her head covered with a white kerchief and with earrings of semi-precious dews, she would sway in the wind, intoxicated with space, light, colour and song.

But now her deep black eyes were without joy, and sad was the song she was singing to the accompaniment of the birds and the wind. Her song was not like any other and seemed to be searching for the road to a distant land. Nargis' heart was reaching out to another heart, one that could understand her and respond to her love with love.

> Unburdened with sorrow
> You are far away, sweet one.
> So who can wipe my tears
> With unquenchable love?
>
> Everyone seeks, at the hour of blossoming,
> The way of union.
> Why have you not set out on that path,
> Why do you hesitate in farness?
>
> There is no harder suffering
> Than ceaseless expectation.
> Come here and dry my tears,
> Come, I crave our hour of meeting!

Resting against a large rock at the foot of the mountain, Nargis closed her deep black eyes that were so full of suffering and sang of her love for Bambur, growing ever louder and more insistent. Swaying in the wind as she sang, this was her expression of her joy and her sadness, and the injury of her solitude. And in moments like this it began to seem to her that the one who so filled her every thought and feeling had suddenly appeared to her out of the midday haze and was coming closer, ever closer, and that his breath was now caressing her silken locks and burning her crimson lips.

The flowers that heard Nargis' song understood that love had taken hold of her entire being and that all her thoughts and feelings were directed solely towards Bambur. Without him she would not see the beauty of the world or drink from the cup of happiness. Because of this she would wait for him, calling for him day after day, hour after hour and instant after instant, for the whole of her life until her eyes were washed over by a wave of grey oblivion. For, no matter how far away her beloved was and how difficult a path she was destined to follow, she believed that sooner or later she would find him and that love would be rewarded by love.

All living things know that such devoted and committed love will sink its roots ever deeper and become an ever-stronger force that neither rapid rivers nor limitless seas, neither scorched-yellow deserts nor high mountains with foothills washed by tumbling streams and peaks hidden in the clouds can hinder. Fearing no trial, it will achieve its goal!

'The goal is distant, Nargis, and your path not easy.
Do you imagine you will reach its end?'
'The way is difficult and arrival uncertain,
Still, only by starting can I hope for my goal.'
'But what if the searing red heat and savage Khorud
Block your way, tear out your petals?
Or your feet are burned by scorching sands,
Or felled by the surge of a river in spate,
Or the tendrils of a whirlwind toss and catch you,
Won't you regret that you took this path?'
'Cruel is the storm and strong, but love's stronger.
Khorud can destroy but has no power over love.
Loving, I will master the mightiest flood;
Loving, I will pass through fire and desert.
A greater danger than Khorud or high waters
Is silence when love bids you go, and singing!'

Nargis' song could be heard all through the valley. The flowers and birds, the breeze and the little streams as they wound their way down from the snowy peaks to the warm earth – they all echoed her. Then another girl joined in her song, a girl whose heart was brimming with ardent dreams of youth and overflowing with all the beauty of which the world was made. And in this way, just as a river is born from a brook and a tree grows from a cutting, young girls in villages far and near joined in response, linked by roads and paths that stretched unbroken to the blue line of the horizon.

Once her voice could no longer be distinguished from the infinity of voices, Nargis danced. All who saw her dancing, now with tender joyfulness and now with inconsolable grief, realised what her situation was, for all things – the birds and the winds, the skies and the seas, the flowers and man – are inextricably connected. Thus it was that Nargis' dreams gave rise to a melody and the melody to the girls' singing; this was then the movement of Nargis' dance, that bewitching dance that brought time to a standstill and drove the flowers to reach up higher and higher.

Finally Nargis grew tired and sat down on a rock.

She was thinking of Bambur. She could not remember when she had first seen him and fallen in love or whether it had been a dream or for real. For is it not so that the boundary between dreaming and wakefulness can grow thinner than the silken thread of a spider's web trembling in the wind, that at moments of happiness you want to pinch yourself – am I asleep? – but in unhappy times the desire arises to wake up? But whatever the reality was, Nargis was consumed by the yearning to see Bambur again, and where and how it had begun no longer mattered.

When a house is on fire there is no time to think about what spark caused it. But if the fire cannot be put out in a day, or two, or three, and it seems that it will never be extinguished, it is possible for one to forget what really happened and to recall things that never happened.

At such moments it began to seem to Nargis that once, in a summer dawn, the sun had extended its rays from the mountain peaks to the foothills like a carpet, and down them came Bambur, surrounded by light. He came down, then stood before her, motionless and in silence, a silence that may have lasted an hour, or a day, or a thousand years – but in any case they could not tear their gaze from one another. Now the flower-filled valley, the celestial mountains and the whole world vanished, melting in Nargis' beautiful eyes, until all that remained was Bambur. And that flower-filled valley and the celestial mountains from which he had descended on the sun's carpet of rays, and all the world vanished, melting in Bambur's great eyes, and all that remained was Nargis.

'I am the King of the Bees,' said Bambur, once he was able to speak. 'How many flower beds and gardens have I flown over, how many mountains and deserts, fertile fields and meadows, but never did I meet anyone like you. Maybe you will not believe me, but I was searching for you. So many years have I searched! There is no corner of this land I haven't searched, not a flower I have not asked, again and again, where are you, where are you? You know, there is a magic mirror of the world that reflects everything that has been, that is and that ever will be. I saw you in it – and ever since then thirst has driven me to seek out the only spring that can quench that thirst. And now I have found that spring – it is you, Nargis. I have found the meaning of my life – it is you. Do not turn me down, for your rejection would be my death, Nargis!'

That is all he said.

But did he really say it? And did he really come down from
to her the mountains, to Nargis? Or was it in fact she who saw him
in the magic mirror of the world?

The line between waking and dream, between the miraculous
and the mundane or between sorcery and creation is gossamer
thin. Perhaps our eyes see more than our mind can grasp; maybe,
dreaming of an apple, we will plant out and grow an orchard.
However this may be, the stream reached the river, the river
reached the sea and love found love. So Bambur came, gliding
down the carpet of sunbeams to kneel at Nargis' feet, to capture
her loving gaze with his own. And whenever he looked away for a
moment, to glimpse the mountains or the valley, Nargis whispered
anxiously:

'No, no, look at me! When you turn away, I feel cold!'

Then when he fell silent, overwhelmed with his feelings, she
urged him: 'No, no, keep talking! When you do not speak, it is as
if the stream has stopped babbling and I wither away in the heat.'

Tears of joy now glistened on her eyelashes like dewdrops at
dawn.

They met at the rock, and the whole valley was filled with blue
and gold light and with contentment and tranquillity. Morning
turned to noon, noon to sunset and the sunset into starry night;
dreams turned into waking and waking into dream. All living

things on earth found harmony, and it seemed that this would go on forever.

But there is no apple that is equally rosy on all sides. No plain that does not lie against mountains or fall away to an abyss. Nor is there goodness that is not stalked by evil.

***

There began to be talk in the valley of a wedding, and all who heard got ready their finest outfits to wear.

But the enemies of all that prospers and thrives, regarding the happiness of life in the valley, grew ever darker with malice and their hatred of Nargis and Bambur increased. Everywhere they had their eyes and ears, invisible to others. As they observed the preparations for the wedding, they resolved to prevent it. They began by curtaining the sky with heavy black clouds. No ray of sunlight could now find its way into the valley by day, nor a single glint of starlight at night.

Yet as he hurried to meet his beloved Bambur never lost his way. Nargis' heart radiated warmth and she shone with light, so he found the way to her without error. The evil forces were infuriated: they sent in putrid air from the bogs and dense mists as grey as wet cotton.

But still Bambur found his way.

Then the dark forces called out: 'Where are you, Whirlwind?

You are a monster among monsters, you are the horror of all horrors. You have thousands of tentacles and you are the eternal enemy of all living things. So come quickly and turn the lands of this valley, near and far, to dust!'

And the Whirlwind set about the task he was given.

The road along which Bambur walked to his trysts was torn up with chasms and fissures; a cloud of grey dust twisted above it and it was impossible to see more than an arm's length away. Only lizards still darted about the ruined road, and scorpions lay in wait behind stones for their prey.

'Well done,' said the forces who ordered the Whirlwind. 'You have served us well. You've broken up the roads – and love without sight of the beloved is like a flower without water. It can water itself with its own tears, but tears will not nourish it but only cause it to wither.'

But malice has only one eye, and even that has a cataract: it can see what lies under its feet, but cannot see around it or into the distance. Nargis' heart cried out, and Bambur still found his way through the clouds of dust.

The dark forces turned next to the Blizzard.

'Now you try – and do it with all your strength. Draw on others for help and let it be seen why you have your formidable name. Whirlwind destroyed the roads of meeting, but that was no use. So show us what you are capable of!'

The Blizzard began to whistle and howl and it was as though

the roof of the world had collapsed. Mountain peaks crumbled and fell as avalanches into the valley, chasms opened up and swallowed streams and rivers whole. All round the valley of flowers, chaos and darkness reigned; it was now a solitary island in a limitless ocean of devastation. And for the first time Bambur, however much he tried, could not find the way to Nargis, and however much Nargis called out to him, he could not hear her.

Instead of Bambur, before Nargis there now stood that shaggy-headed savage the Blizzard, newly dropped out of a black cloud. Crumbs of earth and dust fell off him and there was a smell of burning.

'See how much I love you, Nargis!' he said, fixing her with his eyes that flashed with an ominous fire. 'Look at how much I have managed to do, and it was all for you. But he is no more. He will never be back. Even if he wanted to, he would never be able to come back,' the monster went on, avoiding any mention of Bambur by name. 'Everything around us has been destroyed. All that remains is you and your garden. So be my wife, Nargis!'

Folding up her petals and shaking her head sadly, Nargis said: 'Blizzard, we will never understand each other or be in agreement. Maybe one day the sky will come together with the earth, but kindness and cruelty, war and peace can never be reconciled. So don't try. Even if you make the rivers flow backwards and overturn the mountains, you still won't achieve your aim. Pull up a flower and trample it into the ground if you like – but sooner or later another will grow in its place. And it will bloom, it will blossom! Surround Bambur's roads with fire if you must, but he will still come! Put rocks in his path, let the rivers be seas, but he will overcome the rocks and waves and will come. He will come! Mighty though you are, and able to do much, yet you cannot keep true lovers apart. That is not in your power!

As he listened to Nargis, the Blizzard was filled again with rage, for he was unused to not getting his way. But the flowers that surrounded Nargis, her friends the nightingales and doves, and all who loved and glorified life, made noise and song and cooed with approval. To the Blizzard it seemed that they were all advancing towards him – some of them nodding their brightly-coloured heads and opening their green leaves, and others fluttering and hopping. Bewildered by the persistence and fearlessness of life, the Blizzard did not know what to do next and began to move back. His helpers stopped in wonder, astonished that this force without peer had retreated in the face of the weak.

Nargis continued to speak of beauty and kindness and looked fearlessly into the Blizzard's troubled face. This look burnt into his dark soul with a fire hitherto unknown to him.

And the Blizzard retreated.

Meanwhile on the other side of a rock, the voluptuous tulip Lola rose up and spread out her leaves. She was a friend of Nargis. Wrapped in crimson silk, with purple hues in the shadows and shining with freshness, she was like the smile of a beautiful girl, like that unfathomable combination of lines and colours, imbued with mildness and kindness, about which poems are composed and songs are sung. Her shining eyes were moist and deep; her eyebrows were joined and resembled a swallow in flight. For sure, this was Lola, the child of the dawn! Her dress, her jacket and the hat on her head were born of the sun rising over the horizon and of the snowy mountain peaks; only the sleeves of her dress and her earrings were green like leaves.

All the countless flowers around her greeted her with a bow. If it is arrogant or evil in intent, beauty gives rise to envy and enmity, but if it is kind, beauty gives rise to admiration and reverence.

'I can see you are crying,' said Lola to Nargis. 'What has upset you?'

'The pangs of love are tormenting my heart, and the one who could relieve them is not here,' answered Nargis.

'There is no love without sorrow,' Lola sighed. 'A moment apart is the same as an eternity, and being unable to meet him becomes like death. Yet eternity can again become an instant, and death recedes in the face of hope. So don't grieve. If you hope and believe, Bambur will come. He is probably piercing the darkness now, flying over mountains and deserts, seeking the way to you.'

In grief, the comforting words of a friend are like medicine to an illness. Nargis listened to Lola and grew calmer.

Now the rose Atirgul lifted herself up on the green wave of leaves dancing in the wind. Like all the flowers around her she had blossomed with the returning of spring, opened her buds to the sun in greeting and looked tidy and languid. And now the conversation grew even more trusting and intimate.

The flowers chattered about love and the birds chirped about fidelity. Red poppies gave Nargis comfort, and the trill of nightingales summoned Bambur to the tryst. And as the day grew warmer, their voices grew in strength and the songs rang out ever louder.

> The rustling flowers are never quiet
> In either sun or rain;
> They beautify the garden
> And bless what is about it.
>
> Here Lola, friend to all,
> Shines in the glorious day.
> Companion Atirgul beside her –
> A hundred tongues of flame.
>
> Countless by the river
> Cornflowers crowd and cluster.
> The red makes friends with blue
> Like two lines of a song.

There, where flowers grow
Even dreams can come to life.
The world reveals its fairy tales
There, where flowers grow

Yet nowhere in that land can be
A passion stronger than this:
The certainty of Nargis' love.
How does she live, what can she do?

And the flowers and the birds
And the tumbling mountain streams
With song in honour of her love
Will hasten her time of joy.

So let it be, at the appointed hour
Bambur will hear our song,
That his reflection once again
May fall on Nargis' deep black eyes.

II

So rang out the song in that valley that was both orchard and flower garden, as it were the embodiment of the highest beauty, goodness and harmony. Girls and nightingales, shepherds with pipes, and the breezes – all so different on the face of it, yet here joined in a chorus of many voices.

So it began to seem, as their domains drew closer and began to run together, that the earth and the sky were singing the praises of Nargis' faithfulness and of Bambur's devotion. For all living things know that from the beginning to the end of time, love is the origin of rebirth and renewal in the world.

One who does not know love is a flower that yields no fruit.

One who has no love is a seed that does not sprout.

Once more, shadow came over the valley, the sky filled with dark clouds and a chilling draught descended. An icy whirlwind got up and tore through the valley from one end to the other, sending shivers through the leaves and flowers and coating the buds and petals with poisonous dust. Death, capable of many guises, had come – and in each of them it was death for certain.

It was the Blizzard again, returning with new force and fury.

Goodness bears no grudges and is forgetful, while evil has a long memory.

The Blizzard struck up fire on the rocks and howled, roared and thundered.

But what could the trees do, their tender leaves open like child's palms towards the light? What could the flowers do, fragile on their thin stalks? These children of the sun and clear water, of noble human thought and tender hands, bent low to the ground in the hope of finding cover and at least a little warmth; they hid in hollows and crevices and behind rocks.

This is what Lola also did. And so did Atirgul. And so did Nargis.

So also did the birds, whose song had only recently been sonorous and rich, but which was now a doleful chirping and moaning. For all things are dual in nature, everything has its opposite, and one aspect strives and struggles to change to the other: high and low, light and dark, heat and cold. There had been the hour of joy, and now was the time of tears.

The Blizzard raged on. Formless and shaggy, with thousands of arms and heads, whose enraged eyes now flared up with red and green fire and now were extinguished, he trampled and smashed everything in his path. The son of darkness and wilderness, he brought with him darkness and wilderness, knowing of nothing else and incapable of doing anything else.

In this world, to each is his own: the turtle-dove sings and the hawk kills, warmth grows fruits and grain out of stone, while cold turns crops and fruits to stone, coated with rime. Was it ever different, will it ever be different? The gaze alights on the distant past and it replies, no, it never was different. Reason asks of the future, and it replies: no, it never will be.

And yet, to find out where the road will lead, one must walk along it. And to understand the meaning of a song, one must sing it or hear it to the end.

Though he crossed the length and breadth of the valley time and again, whipping up the streams and causing sand hills to drift, the Blizzard could not find Nargis, however much he stared through his countless crazed eyes. Enraged all the more, he began to brag and threaten:

'Hey, not so fast, you fops, you overdressed moppets in your gaudy rags, where are you? You who imagined you could talk with stars and hold a lion by the mane, did you think you could mess with me? My might has no limit, as the fractured rocks thrown down into the gorge will cry, as streams I have turned back on themselves will babble, as whirlwinds will howl that I have cast up above the clouds! So who else wants to pick a fight with me? Let him show himself! Ah, so you won't talk. Has the thunder of my voice made you dumb? Where are you, Nargis, you giver of life? And where is your Bambur, who is man enough only to fight with butterflies and insects? Come out and submit – or die!'

The Blizzard's raving, ranting and threats were in vain.

The flowers kept silent.

The birds kept silent.

Wisdom does not respond to a maniac's ranting that hears nothing but itself. Nor does life deal with death by bargaining; it fights it or it dies.

The Blizzard howled, screamed, rushed about in his frenzied solitude and began to feel unease, as he did not understand what was going on. It seemed to him that he was doing his utmost, sparing no strength (the limits of which even he did not know) in looking for Nargis, but wherever was she? Had she gone to ground, hiding in some crevice and waiting to return to life later, leaving him helpless to do anything? For sure, living things have such means of saving themselves; for it was in nobody's power to lift up all the earth and mix it with the sky. Still, the Blizzard had accomplices on whom he could call for help. Twisting his shaggy hands into knots and snatching at the snowy peaks, he began to howl:

'Khorud! Hey, Khorud!'

'Why are you shouting?' hissed Khorud, yawning. 'I've just deprived forty villages of their harvest, and I deserve some rest.'

'But don't we help each other out in difficult times? You can kill invisibly; you can penetrate where I cannot break through. You can make roots wither or kill them with cold, you can poison leaves and stems, cause things to rot and send clouds of locusts. Come and help me, kill off what I was unable to finish and turn it into dust for me to scatter.'

'But what about Nargis, for whom you went out of your mind?'

'She rejected me.'

So Khorud came. Or perhaps he crawled, invisible and elusive. Or maybe he swam, passing through the valley bottoms and the lowest places, imperceptible, like a poisonous breath. Everything has its visible aspect that makes it distinguishable from other things. Khorud had millions of such aspects, but rarely appeared in one. When he arrived, everything that had hoped to escape unharmed was at once chewed and crushed in invisible jaws, was drained of blood and dried out, rotted away and crumbled.

'A-ha!' thundered the Blizzard. 'So do you surrender or not?'

From somewhere, faintly, there now came the voice of Nargis, full of suffering. It was impossible to say whether it came from far away or from under the ground:

'No!'

The Blizzard listened for a long time, wondering whether Nargis had really answered or he was merely imagining it.

'Back to work, Khorud,' he decided at length. 'What has been bent must be broken, what is cracked must be crushed.'

Once again, day was turned into night, the sky into a black abyss and the valley into a boiling cauldron. And again Blizzard roared:

'So will you surrender now?'

Perhaps low voices were rising from somewhere unknown like a distant murmur of bees, or maybe it was a barely discernible echo from the past, but either way Blizzard heard:

'No!'

       'No!'

'No!'

III

Now the valley, which until then had been spared for the sake of Nargis, was stripped of its orchards and its gardens; no more were there birds there, nor grass. The springs and streams vanished, the goats and sheep perished and the men who had farmed and shepherded there went away.

Wilderness now stretched in every direction, a place so derelict that people would say that whoever goes there will burn his feet, and any bird that flies there will singe its wings.

Khorud, the old enemy of country folk whose labours feed the human race, the destroyer of trees and devourer of flowers and fruit, sneered: 'Well that's taught them a fine lesson all right!'

For a moment he even became visible – like a gnat that is so scrawny you could almost see through it, yet that after gorging itself on blood becomes almost as large as a bee. Deformed, at once comical and frightening, Khorud looked like nothing on earth. His clothes consisted of dried-out, shredded roots and half-rotted stalks and leaves; he left a trail of crumbs and tatters, and his matted brown hair was teeming with aphids. His eyes were dull and dismal – as though the hunger, disease and suffering he had wreaked on his victims were looking out through them.

'Yes, we did a good job there, it didn't go to waste,' he said to the Blizzard as he regarded the devastated valley. 'Of course, I could have managed it by myself, it wasn't difficult. But when we do these things together it all happens much faster. So shall we go on to other places now and obliterate everything there as well? So that not a single leaf unfolds and no flower opens, so that not a field or forest or garden is left in the world, and no herds of horses or flocks of sheep, no villages and no people. Why do we have these things anyway? I don't like them. Instead let's leave only bare rocks, putrid bogs and scorched deserts.'

'I like your reasoning,' agreed the Blizzard. 'A bare earth gives me more space, I can blow wherever I want. And nobody will defy me, so all power will be in my hands.'

'But what about me?' asked Khorud, worried that Blizzard was thinking only about himself. 'There'll be nothing left for me to do.'

'You'll be able to catch up on your sleep at last and get some rest. You have been at work for centuries.'

'True,' said Khorud, basking in the praise of his accomplice. 'I've done some good work in my time. So now I'll be able to doze all I like. Well, then, shall we go and finish the job straight away?'

'Let me just catch my breath, then, and we'll be off.'

But when Blizzard and Khorud decided to make a final, farewell circle over the valley, to admire what they had achieved, they could not but hear, from somewhere in the depths of the earth where they could not reach, the subdued voice of Nargis. She was singing:

At the bottom of the empty valley
In the warm depths of the earth
The lord is not the Blizzard,
The master is not Khorud.

For those who thirst, a spring
Has arisen from my tears.
If only my beloved
Could press himself to this!

Frost, Blizzard and Khorud
Have all eyes on this valley.
So come and liberate our land:
It is you my desires await.

By these boulders and blue rivers,
Though yet the day seem dark,
I, your ever-burning star
Shall never be extinguished.

A seed, once it falls onto soil, puts out a shoot; the shoot
extends upwards towards the sun and forms a bud, the bud opens
and becomes a flower. The flower lets fall its petals and scatters
seed on the ground. Life is a caravan that moves from oasis to
oasis through gorges and passes, glaciers and deserts. A desert has

an end, but life does not. The voice of evil has an echo that grows weaker with every step until it drops dead, while good is the source of legend and song – and these are again like caravans travelling from oasis to oasis, like seed travelling to seed through bud and flower, and through the soul and memory of the generations they reach eternity.

Nargis survived in the depths of the earth.

Nargis was being restored to life.

Nargis was singing.

Hearing her, other flowers responded to her singing; the bravest of them soon raised their heads from the ground and now, though still cautiously, the valley broke out once more in colour.

'What's all this?' wondered Khorud, shivering with cold. 'And where has it come from?'

Having expended all his strength, the Blizzard sighed and said nothing.

But the flowers talked among themselves in songs.

Nargis
Dear friends! The storms of days gone by
Have united us and made us stronger!

Lola
Yes, not the Blizzard, nor ugly Khorud
Can take away life's light or colours!

Atirgul
The foe will retreat, and from my cheek
I'll rub the dust, again I'll wear crimson silk!

Navruzgul²
The evil has passed. The skies grow light,
and our leaves are washed clean by the dew!

Nargis
Once more I hear the rustling of leaves.
O sing of life, O garden of the spring!

---

2 *Navruzgul* – a flower worn by girls at celebrations
(such as Navruz, the Persian New Year).

IV

'Do you hear that?' said Khorud again. 'What is it?'

'They've come back to life, that's what it is', hissed the Blizzard.

'But what for?'

'Spring is coming.'

'I don't know what that is and don't want to know. My business is to destroy.'

'Well, spring brings warmth, heals illness and brings the lifeless to life.'

'So does this mean that all our efforts were wasted?' Khorud was angry. 'Does it mean that the whole valley will be full of these garish rags again and they'll make fun of us?'

The Blizzard, sullen and weary, flared up at Khorud's last words:

'Why are you getting all fretful now, Khorud? Why have you gone soft? It's true, I have fewer assistants now, as the frost, the snow and the ice have gone up to the mountaintops. But the rain, the hail, the whirlwinds, the thunder, the lightning and the chilling fogs are still here. The flowers and grass are still weak, they haven't regained their strength yet. And your hordes, Khorud, are on their way – the hot winds that can dry sap, the beetles, the worms and greenfly. They are beyond counting! We'll prove ourselves yet, trust me! So they are waiting for sunshine? We'll make them wait – I'll bring dark clouds down on the valley again. They want warmth? Let's give them cold rain, hit them with hail, dazzle them with lightning and trample them into the ground. Are they waiting for moths to come and fly above them like a living rainbow? Are they waiting for bumblebees to come and fly from flower to flower, singing songs as they go? Well, set the insects on them that sting, gnaw and chew, that undermine the roots of trees and drink dry the sap. Come on, Khorud, let's give it another try!'

Dawn began to brighten, but in the valley nobody could see it – the sky was covered with clouds.

The sun rose, but in the valley nobody could see it – it illuminated only the peaks that stood above the clouds.

The day began, but in the valley it was still twilight.

Now the heavens opened: from end to end of the valley rushed swollen streams of water that bent the flowers and grasses to the ground.

Hail then came on them, beating like a drum roll, hopping and stretching into oblique threads that twisted into tight white ropes, trampling stalks, leaves and petals.

The thunder clapped and burst as though giving out a warning: 'Hey, all of you, get out of my way, I will smash you and grind you into dust!'

From out of the black clouds slithered tongues of lightning, seething like gigantic snakes with fiery scales.

Everywhere, beetles and bark beetles, caterpillars, greenflies, rot and mould were crawling and spreading.

In the villages people said: 'Foul weather yet again! What offence have we committed before heaven?'

The flowers wilted and fell silent, half-dead, their colours faded. Drained of all her strength, Nargis lay out on the ground.

Sometimes it seems that happiness is on your threshold, but when you look closer, you see misfortune peering over its shoulder.

Sometimes it appears that the road ahead, open to the horizon, is level and easy, but when you start out along it you come across pits and openings in which you might break not only your legs but also your head. Only the wisdom of old age remembers always that both the nightingale and the black kite fly out of their nests on one and the same day; that both wheat and thorn-bushes that even a donkey would refuse grow in the same field. But young flowers believe that they germinate and grow for joy alone. Alas! If only the seeds could tell the new shoots and flowers everything they knew! But the flower dies when the seed is formed, and when a new flower emerges, there remains of the seed only a husk. They become one another, but can never meet – that is the law.

Flattened against the ground, battered by hail and soiled with silt, the flowers had scarcely revived before the life began to ebb from them once more.

Nargis lay prostrate beside a rock, the remnants of her strength fading.

But the bringers of the bad weather and misfortune were celebrating.

Blizzard
How strong you are, Khorud! So cunning you are, old man!
Unseen and unheard, you came and wiped them all out!
For all your exploits I'll let you choose reward –
Whatever you wish, I'll gladly grant.
For your courage and accomplishment in war,
What prize would you have? Brocades? Silk? A wife?

Khorud
But what more do I need?
I am wholly satisfied
With but a single reward –
This country barren and laid to waste.

Blizzard
Khorud, the flower garden's dead. But the roots remain.
Move through the earth, the hour of revenge await.
I cannot reach them there – but from your hordes
Choose who can reach them and bring them to their end.

'Well, and what about you?' asked Khorud. 'So again I must set to, sparing no strength, while you rest? You want me to prepare the meal while you put out the spoons?'

'Come on, now,' said the Blizzard. 'The one who walks at the rear of the caravan has to swallow the most dust, but is also last to drink from the spring. I need Nargis. Dead or alive. I'm with you, but I have no power over those who take refuge.'

For two more days the winds raged over the valley, the thunder roared, the lightning seared and the rains brought floods. And for two more days and two more nights the blind and the bulging-eyed, the legless and those with forty legs, the long, like needles, and the rotund, like balls, the stinging, chewing helpers of Khorud fumbled about the surface and penetrated into the soil. And when it was all over, the Blizzard stopped above the prostrate Nargis.

Her eyes were closed and her eyebrows were still, but she was breathing and her heart was beating. It beat slowly, unsteadily and wearily, but still, it beat.

Some say that death is stronger than anything or anybody. O people, if you say this, then look around and tell me – if death is stronger than all else, why is it that wheat comes into ear, why do the grasses rustle and the forests give a blue haze, why do herds of horses and flocks of sheep roam? Why do the villages multiply and cities arise? Life is a fire and death is ashes, but rake over any pile of ashes that looks to have cooled long ago into grey oblivion, and a spark will light up and a crumb of charcoal will twinkle and give rise to a new flame.

'Finish her off,' said Khorud, 'Or let me do it. What use is she to you like this?'

The Blizzard wanted to say that he would do it himself, but again he was fixed, stunned by Nargis' beauty. He stopped, bewildered: what was happening to him? Had he turned to life itself for advice, life would have explained – but whenever did a murderer stop and ask advice of his victim?

And as the Blizzard stood stupefied, he heard a whisper:

'Bambur, King of the Bees! I'm waiting for you! Waiting for you! Waiting…'

Khorud and the Blizzard began to worry, for they could expect no good out of Bambur. If he were alone, they could overcome him; but they knew that he had innumerable hosts of helpers. One bee by itself is small, its wings are weak, but when they are together in millions they can unleash a whirlwind that breaks trees and shakes rocks. A bee's sting burns like fire; each bee has only one sting, but when they come at their victim in a great cloud, even a giant will collapse in death agonies as though attacked by spears and swords, cursing the day and the hour when he challenged Bambur.

Little things, grains, drops – what are they really? A grain of sand is small, yet of such grains are the mountains made on which the clouds and stars take rest. A drop of water is small, but the sea that crushes rocks and brings ships to grief is composed of drops.

'Poor Nargis,' said the Blizzard, looking around him just in case. 'You are calling for Bambur in vain; they say he's already dead. And anyway, what could he have done by himself against those who can turn day into night, stop rivers and change the colour of the earth from green to black and yellow? The world is ruled by power, and that power is me. But power needs tenderness for repose and joy, and that tenderness is you. So why don't we unite this power and this tenderness?'

'But where, Blizzard, have you seen a friendship or union between ice and fire? Yes, you are power, but you are the power of death, cold and darkness. And I am the power of love – the power of warmth, light and joy.'

'And what sort of a power are you, if you are lying flat and calling for help?'

'Well, what kind of power are you if you could not deal with us by yourself and needed to call on your friend Khorud?'

'Your words are too bold, Nargis. The words of the vanquished must be praise for the victor.'

'The one defeated is neither a captive nor a slave while his spirit is free.'

'Then he is a corpse.'

'Are you threatening me again?'

'I gave you the right to choose.'

'Well, kill me then.'

'Life, Nargis, is the greatest delight that exists in this world. Death is silence, cold and emptiness.'

'Don't try to tempt me and don't try to intimidate me.'

'I am telling you the truth.'

'No. You are dressing up your untruths in the garb of truth. The truth is that there is no life without love, the truth is that those who betray love are betraying life. You can go on humiliating me by all means, you can obliterate me, but remember: in my love I will be revived, in my love I will rise again!'

The Blizzard was seized by complex feelings, from astonishment to fury. How could such a creature, that looked so weak and helpless, display such determination, resolve and self-sacrifice? Or was there really something in the world that he, although he had raged over its lands for century after century, did not know and did not understand? Why no, of course not, he reasoned – it was just chatter, trifles and foolish stubbornness. Only power had ever ruled the world or would ever do so. The one who is strong is the ruler, the one who is strong dictates his will over all the others.

'Very well, then, don't take offence,' said the Blizzard. 'You have chosen your own fate. But I will not kill you straight away – there is no hurry. No, instead I'll watch as you gradually approach, moment by moment in pain and torment, the line beyond which there's only darkness and the abyss! They say that waiting for death is worse than dying itself – well, you'll find out…'

***

Bambur, meanwhile, was looking for the way to where Nargis was, but could not find it. The road had been covered with dust and sand by the Whirlwind, pecked apart by hail and washed away by streams sent by the Blizzard; Khorud had crawled along it as he went about levelling everything under the dismal colour of the wasteland. Before, there had been springs along the way as clear as the eyes of cranes, whose babbling indicated to him the direction to go, but now they had been blocked and filled with lumps of rock and earth. The mountain peaks that used to guide him were covered by swirling clouds. There used to be a small river that ran down the middle of the road, cheering him and indicating the way, but now it flowed backwards, between different, changed banks, passing in places through flooded fields and meadows.

He called out to the eagle: 'Respond to me!' He summoned the star: 'Show yourself!' and he asked the wind: 'Disperse these clouds!' But the eagles shrank back into clefts in the rocks; the star could not break through the clouds; and the wind, unable to control itself, merely hurled itself one way and the other, not knowing why.

Bambur had grown thinner and worn himself out with suffering, yet had not lost hope. He walked straight ahead and so overcame the chaos and darkness. And one day he addressed a plea to the sun:

65

O sun, where are you? Show yourself!
In the darkness you gave birth to life –
So why have you forgotten us now?
Look down and make visible the roads.
Help me find my Nargis, hear me, pray –
That girl who's so deeply in love!

The suffering I feel is beyond the telling,
My search is hard and my enemy crafty.
The distances grow stormy and dark as a grave,
So let your rays, dear sun, fall again on the land,
Show me the way and return to me
That girl who's so deeply in love!

For me she's the beginning and end
Of all the hopes and joys of this world –
Without her, my strength leaks away.
Illuminate for me the difficult road,
Help me bring back my Nargis so sweet,
That girl who's so deeply in love!

The sun has much to do and it receives many requests – some
of them unwise or contradictory.
In one place, where the ground was saturated with rain and

pierced with cold, the sun was asked to shine, to warm the ground and grow crops and grass.

In another place, where there had been no rain for a long time, they asked it to go from the sky, to stop torturing and burning, because a scorched earth brought famine and pestilence.

In one place people turn their faces to the sun so that it caresses the skin and smooths out wrinkles, while in another, people cover their faces and hide in the shade. So even if it wished, the sun could never please everybody.

But love has a special voice that ascends to the skies, penetrates deep underground and crosses oceans and seas. Neither raging waves nor a typhoon can quash it.

The sun heard Bambur; moved by his suffering, it decided to help. It threw tongues of fire and poured avalanches of heat and light onto the thick clouds, forcing them to part. Not for long, to be sure. But long enough for Bambur to see his way, and he made a dash for the valley with the speed of an arrow released from a strong man's bow.

As he ran, he heard through the howling wind and the rush of the streams the voice of Nargis, filled with suffering.

Eventually Bambur reached the valley, but, looking round, he did not recognise it. 'Am I really mistaken again?' he wondered. For what he could see was not the valley of flowers and life that he knew; what he saw was a valley of destruction, desolation and death. Where were the flowers and grasses that once carpeted it from end to end and swayed in the summer breeze, like yellow, blue, red, orange and purple butterflies that whirled about in intricate dances?

Instead of this were only black and brown patches, gullies, sand hills and balls and tangles of shredded roots and stalks.

Where were the subtle and intoxicating fragrances that no word in any language could describe?

There were none. The only smells were of dust, rotting and decay.

Where were the innumerable songs of countless birds, their whistling, warbling and trilling, to which the moon listened spellbound in the pre-dawn sky, as did the dazzling white clouds in the heat of midday? Where was the rustling of the petals, the leaves, the stems, the blades of grass and the branches as they greeted one another and told each other about everything that was happening in the valley, outside the valley and in the distant lands beyond the reach of sight?

There were none. There was only the hoarse noise of a deathly wind and the toneless howling of the Blizzard like a dog in some faraway gorge.

If he had been able, Bambur would have wept tears of grief and despair. But he was unable to weep and thereby relieve his soul.

If he had been able, he would have cursed the laws of heaven and earth that allowed the humiliation of the weak by the strong and permitted injustice, destruction and the mocking of goodness by evil.

But he could not curse. He could only feel sympathy and compassion and help others.

He sat down sadly on a rock and began to sing, for only in singing can the mind and soul pour themselves out fully and unite the past with the present and action with dream.

> Asking to be shown the way
> I've come from distant lands
> To look for you, to find you
> Nargis, my beloved!
>
> Where are you? Where are you?
> All about are but fissures and hills,
> Dark and empty, piles of dust.
> Where are the birds and the flowers now?
>
> They closed their eyes,
> They silenced their voices,
> And overhead, the leaden sky
> As sullen as the grave.
>
> Who was it, what was he like,
> The mastermind behind this theft?
> So at home with brutality that he plays
> Games with others' destinies?

Maybe you, Khorud, were involved,
This project and labour were yours?
Or maybe you, blind Blizzard, were behind
This unfair trial, this dirty work?

So why are you so silent now,
You lions with hearts of sheep?
Come now and fight! Ere long
You'll each have your price to pay.

Come now and fight! Face me and fight!
And springtime, you faithful aide,
Be quick! Grieve not, Nargis –
I'll see you soon, my bride!

What is a song? Some people believe it to be no more than a pleasant form of idleness. The thoughts of such people are without wings and their hearts are encrusted with rind. Others think that singing is a way of baring one's soul so that it is made known to others. These people see with only one eye and hear with only one ear. Others again consider that a song carries the wisdom of the mind and soul, and that it makes the sap move faster in the tree and the blood run faster in the veins. They say that song makes the weak strong in an unequal fight, and the timid brave. It is not the one whose position looks hopeless who is doomed, but rather the one who cannot sing his own song. Who cannot at least sing it to himself, in his heart, without words!

So Bambur sang. It would be impossible to try to repeat everything that his song contained. Anyway, who knows how many ordinary words can be replaced by one word of song? Has anybody measured how many years and miles, hopes and actions are contained in a single line of song? Or counted how many life-giving forces are born from an idea that has become an image and music at the same time?

Many have endeavoured to understand, but given up with only crumbs of truth that would not feed a sparrow.

Bambur sang: and the valley became quieter and quieter. Bambur sang, and in the valley it became lighter and warmer.

How long did this go on? Nobody knows. It may be that time itself, hearing the song, lost track of itself; maybe, spellbound and on wing, it moved at the speed of a stream that falls from a high precipice to the bottom of a gorge. Still, as Bambur sang, changes began to occur in the valley – at first scarcely perceptibly, but gradually faster and more evident.

Exhaling and exuding a gentle steam, the earth began to move. Here and there, like fledglings emerging from the nest, new shoots put out their first pairs of leaves. Gleaming with droplets of dew and lengthening upwards, they then formed buds with an artistry so inconceivable that the greatest sculptor would be envious.

What a wonder is growth! Millennia have passed and millennia will pass, yet however much we may come to understand the mystery of being, we will always be astounded by the fact that from dull and ordinary earth, and sometimes from between bare stones, tender leaves appear, and later, flowers whose richness and variety of colour exceeds the glories of rainbows and the dawn. They are at once the children of the earth, the sun and the stars!

The moment arrived: the buds became flowers.
And Lola dressed in crimson nodded her head:
'Greetings, Bambur! We were waiting for you!'
Intoxicating with fragrance, Atirgul murmured:
'Greetings, Bambur! We are glad to see you.'
And the flowers took up Bambur's song:

The troubles of the hour of exhaustion are gone,
Once more the valley is full of life.
Glory to you for waking us,
Glory to you, O spring!

Evil forces do not sleep,
We know they are biding their time.
Let fields and gardens return to life,
And flower upon flower revive.

From heaven let Blizzard and Khorud,
Subverted, fall forever and from power.
Let nightingales in a blaze of summer lightning
Sing praises to the spring!

For sure, not everything had yet returned to its earlier form, and the valley was only beginning to come back to life. There were still clouds in the sky, albeit thinner now, and broken. Storm clouds could still be seen on the horizon, with gleams of lightning issuing from them, but they were at a distance and not so alarming. Everything was alive again and full of hope. But what in fact is hope? Hope is the image of a thing that does not exist but that will come into existence if we apply effort. For the one who swims without having a definite goal or having striven for the path will find himself in a place he did not intend to reach and discover what he had not been seeking.

If you are crossing a turbulent stream, lean on the staff of hope.
If you are descending into a dark gorge, light the torch of hope.
If your heart is withered by misfortune, drink from the spring of hope.

V

Nargis, who had put all her remaining energy into her call to Bambur, was lying behind a rock in a semi-conscious state. She could hear Bambur singing, but it seemed to her to be far distant and she thought: 'I'm probably asleep and dreaming. Or else Bambur knows nothing of our tribulations and is singing somewhere else, and the echo is playing tricks on me.' She could sense through her closed eyelids that the valley was growing lighter, but she thought: 'When we dream, our wishes take on a visible aspect and walk on the earth. It seems to me as though day is dawning. But I expect it's just the Blizzard – he's probably struck a rock with lightning or something.' Then she heard Lola and Atirgul greeting Bambur, but thought: 'The person we love is always with us and inside us. This is probably just my memory, speaking in their voices'.

And she sighed.

And Bambur heard her sigh, turned, and saw her.

When two lovers meet after a long and painful separation, you should look away.

Anybody who has experienced love even long ago is aware that at that moment, even friends' eyes are not wanted.

All who are in the happy years of their youth will understand that at the moment of the long-awaited meeting, even the eyes of brothers and sisters should keep away.

And those for whom the joy of love is still ahead will realise, when their time comes, that even the eyes of their mother and father had best be averted.

Nobody can say what happens to the sky, the stars, the sun, the earth, the trees, the birds and the flowers when the two lovers meet – but at that moment they, he and she, are alone in the world.

'How much you have gone through in waiting for me!' said Bambur.

'And how much have you endured in looking for me!' replied Nargis.

'I would go ten times as far only to see you again', exclaimed Bambur.

'And I would endure ten times more only to see you again,' sighed Nargis.

She looked at him with her beautiful almond eyes, and they said more to him than all the books, legends and fairy-tales created since the beginning of time could contain. Tenderly he placed his hands on her shoulders; their trembling said more to her than all the books, legends and fairy-tales to the end of time could contain.

And once they had said enough and said no more, once they had told each other everything and no longer uttered a word and once they had promised each other that they would always be together and had no promises left to make, then the blue sky and the springtime sun returned to their places, the earth once more took on its dappled greens and the water in the streams resumed its babbling.

> Make noise, O spring, and sing, my heart!
> Washed clean with daylight and the dew,
> In the name of love and friendship we
> Come fresh to the dawn of this given day.
>
> Unsleeping chirps the nightingale
> In some cool glade of green,
> The son of cloud and glacier worlds
> Now babbles in a pebble creek.
>
> Countless are we who now rejoice,
> But somewhere evil forces lurk.
> Quiet now, they await their time,
> Unseen, they ready their revenge.
>
> Our bonds of friendship are our answer.
> Here not everyone is weak, but none.
> High above, the stars look small –
> But perpetual is their glittering light!

From a dark gorge into which the sun does not shine and whose walls are covered with a pallid moss, Khorud and the

Blizzard looked on as the valley came back to life.

'Do you hear that?' said Khorud in his hoarse voice. 'Those gaudy rags with their spindly legs, whose veins carry only water – they've got it into their heads yet again that the valley is theirs. Well, Blizzard, what do you make of it?'

> *Blizzard*
> He won't survive the end of the day
> Who rises up to oppose me.
> Summit peaks and waves of the sea
> Have submitted to my forces.

'That's all fair enough,' agreed Khorud, 'I saw how you smashed the waves, throwing them onto the shore, and how you tore the white caps off the mountains and hurled them into the valleys. And the tongue can't argue with a witness like the eyes. But now my eyes tell me that the grass, the flowers and the trees of the valley are getting ever closer to us. Now I can kill too, of course, though not in a single charge, like you. Instead, I do it gradually, little by little, one at a time if need be. But I think that there are too many of them again, and they are getting stronger.'

> I can strike and bring them down,
> Cut short the thread of life.
> I've fought for longer than an age,
> So why is that thread so tough?

'That's just it, Khorud,' grumbled the Blizzard with exasperation. 'You certainly sent plenty of them to the next world without making much fuss. But what use was it? Look at the valley now – there seem to be more of them than ever!'

'Right, and the sea has not overflowed onto the land as you were threatening,' hinted Khorud caustically. 'And the mountain tops are wearing their white caps again…'

'It looks as if we're about to have another argument,' said the Blizzard. 'But what for? When the strong quarrel, they give strength to the weak. We'd do better to listen to what they are chattering about down there. Maybe there's something secret in all this that we don't know about?'

But this is what they were saying in the valley:

Navruzgul
This world is peopled with good and ill alike.
Who of these is weak and who is strong?
No need for words, they hold no answer –
Just look in the valley, you'll find it there.

Lola
Again to bloom, once more my costume's red
Again the noontime blazes overhead.
What fear I if Blizzard lets out rumours?
He's the one that withered; I'm alive!

Atirgul
There was darkness and wind, lightning and hail
But now once more I exude my scent.
It makes friendships stronger a hundred times,
But for my enemies it's poison and hell!

Bambur
Well here it is, the wonderful time has come
For happiness, goodness and joy at last.
Should Blizzard or Khorud show their face
We'll have them – they'll not come out alive!

'Well, how do you like that?' said Khorud, once the songs began to die down. 'They're even threatening us!'

'I acknowledge power,' said the Blizzard after thinking for a while. 'But maybe many small powers, when they act all for one and one for all, also add up to a great power. And Bambur is with them, and he can summon so many bees, bumblebees and wasps that they would black out the sky.'

Now there appeared on the mountain slopes, along the roads and in the gardens by the villages a white light that spread ever wider, in places taking on a pinkish tinge. In those places it was as though dawn was breaking over fallen snow. And on the edge of the valley, its twigs inclined towards it, there rose a tree that resembled a swirling, snow-white cloud.

'What do you reckon that means?' wondered the Blizzard.

'Not good news,' mumbled Khorud, who crawled over and ransacked the ground more often and knew it better. 'That is Yavun the apricot tree. They say it has a miraculous hardiness, and certainly I've broken my teeth on it more than once. Don't bother getting mixed up with it. And look, behind it are pomegranate and almond trees, all of them blossoming and rising to the sky. Not even cliffs can stop them – they climb up from ledge to ledge, clutching at everything that can be clutched, provided there is sun and water.'

'And can they reach us?'

'Who knows? There was a time when they lived only near the villages, but now you can see how far they reach. And look, look, there are more and more of them – they're moving, they're travelling in waves, higher and higher!'

The Blizzard looked out on the valley and foothills that girdled it. Everywhere he could cast his eyes he saw either rippling grasses of many colours or trees in blossom that curled and ascended the slopes. Sometimes, gusts of wind blew petals from them, that floated down like tiny moths, glimmers of pink and white, suddenly flashing as they caught rays of sunlight, before circling and descending onto roads and paths, or rising towards the clouds. And now the Blizzard felt that his power was fading, seeping away from him like water from a mountain lake after its dam has burst. He began to contract and to shrink until he resembled a black python; at this he slid down from the cliff, seethed and squirmed on the rocks and crawled up into a gorge, where he found a dark, narrow crevice.

'That's not the end of me!' he hissed. 'Just wait until they're tired and they start to quarrel. Then I'll be back!'

'And what about me?' called out Khorud after him. 'Why are you leaving me alone?'

But the Blizzard did not reply. Having reached his dark place, he crawled in, coiled himself up into a ball and sank into oblivion.

Khorud remained alone. He also felt exhausted and sick, but the curse that hung over him drove him harder and harder until, afraid to go down into the valley, he threw himself onto some slimy grey moss that oozed water and hung by threads from the walls of the gorge.

And the valley was filled with rejoicing!

The flowers and grasses formed a great round dance of many circles, braided and interwoven, in which all the colours of the valley ran brightly, in which all the voices of the valley called to one another; that dance overflowed into the gardens on all sides and onto the slopes of the mountains.

'Greetings, O bearer of nectar!' said Bambur to Yavun. 'We know you are here to show us the way to sunlight and warm rain!'

'Greetings, Yavun!', added Lola. 'If you have a fiancée, I will give her my petal, which will be like a flaming red fire on her white dress!'

'Greetings, Yavun!' whispered Atirgul. 'If you have a bride, I will give her the best perfume in the world!'

And Yavun, who looked like a snow-white cloud, replied:

> The powers of sorcery have faded,
> And spring illuminates the way.
> Nargis has let her dark curls
> Fall on Bambur's strong chest.
>
> The sun shines in the firmament,
> Warm and full race the rivers.
> May there be for all of us this day
> Freedom, harmony and love!

VI

Some say that spring is the awakening of life. This was probably an idea thought up by a poet who imagined the winter snow as a downy quilt. In the early dawn it takes the form of a beautiful girl who washes herself with cold water and gives him a radiant smile.

Others say that spring is the continuation of life. Most likely this was the thoughts of a ploughman as he gathered seed from one harvest to grow for the next.

Another view is that spring is the awakening of life for its continuation and renovation. This was surely decided by a wise man with a grey beard, who united the poet's reverie and the ploughman's experience and joined them with the great and mysterious quality that life has of reawakening after stagnation or shock, of continuing by means of seeds and roots and of perpetually renewing itself in searching and daring. This is not an easy path; it is full of dangers and misfortune, yet in the place where one ear of wheat once grew, two more will grow, and in the place where there stood a bush, a tree will grow, extending its roots into the cool depths and straining its top into the hot sky.

In the valley where Nargis and Bambur had met there came awakening, continuation and renovation. Now it looked like a magnificent suzani, which to a fool was no more than a piece of cloth, but for one with intelligence it told a tale of being and recited a poem of love, written by the hands of nature in the language of nature!

If you can read it – then read!

Epilogue

It was in Kashmir.

We were sailing in a steamer along the Jhelum river. It was there that we first heard this song about Nargis and Bambur, sung first on the main deck by our travelling companions, and then later on the bank, performed by our generous hosts. The song was accompanied by folk melodies played on ancient national instruments.

Many people greeted us, friends of our country: 'Your visit brings joy for us'. They told us that all kinds of people sing this song – arable farmers, shepherds, workers in the towns and craftsmen. And they each gave it a different shade of interpretation.

For the young, inexperienced in life, it was simply a song about love and spring.

For those with a philosophical bent it was a reflection of a pantheistic vision of nature rooted in the distant past, but it was also a figurative and musical interpretation of what constantly takes place all around us – the changing of the seasons, regrowth from seeds and the struggle between good and evil forces.

Others said thoughtfully: 'You know, Blizzard is well suited to personify the oppression and enslavement that our people endured for so long, while Khorud aptly represents a petty colonial official, the type that came here in swarms and sucked away our wealth one crumb at a time.'

I myself cannot identify with any particular commentary on the tale, nor do I seek a generalisation. That will always be left to the discretion of those whose forefathers composed the song, whose grandfathers and fathers carried it into our own time and who perform it today. In my view, the deeper, wider and more majestic a river is, the more it can reflect and the more beautiful it is.

That is the reason why I decided to retell this song, although I do not doubt for a moment that something has been lost; that it can only ever subsist in its fullness and harmony in the language in which it was created and in which it is performed.

Finally, I would like this to be an expression of my gratitude to my Kashmiri and Indian friends. Our time together will remain forever in my memory.

Singapore – Delhi – Tashkent
December 1955 – August 1976, 1977